P9-DCX-279

EXISTENTIALISM
AND HUMAN EMOTIONS

EXISTENTIALISM
and
HUMAN EMOTIONS

BY

JEAN-PAUL SARTRE

THE WISDOM LIBRARY

A *Division of*

PHILOSOPHICAL LIBRARY
New York

Distributed to the trade by
Citadel Press, Inc.
A subsidiary of Lyle Stuart, Inc.
120 Enterprise Avenue
Secaucus, New Jersey 07094

COPYRIGHT 1957 BY PHILOSOPHICAL LIBRARY, INC.
15 EAST 40TH STREET, NEW YORK 16, N. Y.

ALL RIGHTS RESERVED

Printed in the United States of America

ISBN 0-8065-0902-3

The section on "Existentialism" is taken from the book of that name, translated by Bernard Frechtman; all other selections are from *Being and Nothingness,* translated by Hazel E. Barnes.

CONTENTS

EXISTENTIALISM
AND HUMAN EMOTIONS

EXISTENTIALISM

I SHOULD LIKE on this occasion to defend existentialism against some charges which have
been brought against it.

First, it has been charged with inviting people to remain in a kind of desperate quietism
because, since no solutions are possible, we
should have to consider action in this world as
quite impossible. We should then end up in a
philosophy of contemplation; and since contemplation is a luxury, we come in the end to
a bourgeois philosophy. The communists in
particular have made these charges.

On the other hand, we have been charged
with dwelling on human degradation, with
pointing up everywhere the sordid, shady, and
slimy, and neglecting the gracious and beauti-
ful, the bright side of human nature; for example, according to Mlle. Mercier, a Catholic
critic, with forgetting the smile of the child.
Both sides charge us with having ignored human solidarity, with considering man as an
isolated being. The communists say that the
main reason for this is that we take pure subjectivity, the *Cartesian I think,* as our starting
point; in other words, the moment in which

man becomes fully aware of what it means to him to be an isolated being; as a result, we are unable to return to a state of solidarity with the men who are not ourselves, a state which we can never reach in the *cogito*.

From the Christian standpoint, we are charged with denying the reality and seriousness of human undertakings, since, if we reject God's commandments and the eternal verities, there no longer remains anything but pure caprice, with everyone permitted to do as he pleases and incapable, from his own point of view, of condemning the points of view and acts of others.

I shall try today to answer these different charges. Many people are going to be surprised at what is said here about humanism. We shall try to see in what sense it is to be understood. In any case, what can be said from the very beginning is that by existentialism we mean a doctrine which makes human life possible and, in addition, declares that every truth and every action implies a human setting and a human subjectivity.

As is generally known, the basic charge against us is that we put the emphasis on the dark side of human life. Someone recently told me of a lady who, when she let slip a vulgar word in a moment of irritation, excused herself by saying, "I guess I'm becoming an exis-

tentialist." Consequently, existentialism is re-
garded as something ugly; that is why we are
said to be naturalists; and if we are, it is rather
surprising that in this day and age we cause so
much more alarm and scandal than does nat-
uralism, properly so called. The kind of person
who can take in his stride such a novel as Zola's
The Earth is disgusted as soon as he starts read-
ing an existentialist novel; the kind of person
who is resigned to the wisdom of the ages—
which is pretty sad—finds us even sadder. Yet,
what can be more disillusioning than saying
"true charity begins at home" or "a scoundrel
will always return evil for good"?

We know the commonplace remarks made
when this subject comes up, remarks which always add up to the same thing: we shouldn't
struggle against the powers-that-be; we
shouldn't resist authority; we shouldn't try to
rise above our station; any action which
doesn't conform to authority is romantic; any
effort not based on past experience is doomed
to failure; experience shows that man's bent
is always toward trouble, that there must be a
strong hand to hold him in check, if not,
there will be anarchy. There are still people
who go on mumbling these melancholy old
saws, the people who say, "It's only human!"
whenever a more or less repugnant act is
pointed out to them, the people who glut

themselves on *chansons réalistes;* these are the
people who accuse existentialism of being too
gloomy, and to such an extent that I wonder
whether they are complaining about it, not
for its pessimism, but much rather its opti-
mism. Can it be that what really scares them in
the doctrine I shall try to present here is that
it leaves to man a possibility of choice? To answer this question, we must re-examine it on a
strictly philosophical plane. What is meant by
the term *existentialism?*

Most people who use the word would be
rather embarrassed if they had to explain it,
since, now that the word is all the rage, even
the work of a musician or painter is being
called existentialist. A gossip columnist in
Clartés signs himself *The Existentialist,* so that
by this time the word has been so stretched
and has taken on so broad a meaning, that it no
longer means anything at all. It seems that for
want of an advance-guard doctrine analogous
to surrealism, the kind of people who are eager
for scandal and flurry turn to this philosophy
which in other respects does not at all serve
their purposes in this sphere.

Actually, it is the least scandalous, the most
austere of doctrines. It is intended strictly for
specialists and philosophers. Yet it can be defined easily. What complicates matters is that

there are two kinds of existentialist; first, those who are Christian, among whom I would include Jaspers and Gabriel Marcel, both Catholic; and on the other hand the atheistic existentialists, among whom I class Heidegger, and then the French existentialists and myself. What they have in common is that they think that existence precedes essence, or, if you prefer, that subjectivity must be the starting point.

Just what does that mean? Let us consider some object that is manufactured, for example, a book or a paper-cutter: here is an object which has been made by an artisan whose inspiration came from a concept. He referred to the concept of what a paper-cutter is and likewise to a known method of production, which is part of the concept, something which is, by and large, a routine. Thus, the paper-cutter is at once an object produced in a certain way and, on the other hand, one having a specific use; and one can not postulate a man who produces a paper-cutter but does not know what it is used for. Therefore, let us say that, for the paper-cutter, essence—that is, the ensemble of both the production routines and the properties which enable it to be both produced and defined—precedes existence. Thus, the presence of the paper-cutter or book in front of me is determined. Therefore, we have here a technical view of the world whereby it can be said that production precedes existence.

When we conceive God as the Creator, He is generally thought of as a superior sort of artisan. Whatever doctrine we may be considering, whether one like that of Descartes or that of Leibnitz, we always grant that will more or less follows understanding or, at the very least, accompanies it, and that when God creates He knows exactly what He is creating. Thus, the concept of man in the mind of God is comparable to the concept of paper-cutter in the mind of the manufacturer, and, following certain techniques and a conception, God produces man, just as the artisan, following a definition and a technique, makes a paper-cutter. Thus, the individual man is the realization of a certain concept in the divine intelligence.

In the eighteenth century, the atheism of the *philosophes* discarded the idea of God, but not so much for the notion that essence precedes existence. To a certain extent, this idea is found everywhere; we find it in Diderot, in Voltaire, and even in Kant. Man has a human nature; this human nature, which is the concept of the human, is found in all men, which means that each man is a particular example of a universal concept, man. In Kant, the result of this universality is that the wild-man, the natural man, as well as the bourgeois, are circumscribed by the same definition and have the same basic qualities. Thus, here too the essence of man precedes the historical existence that we find in nature.

Atheistic existentialism, which I represent, is more coherent. It states that if God does not exist, there is at least one being in whom existence precedes essence, a being who exists before he can be defined by any concept, and that this being is man, or, as Heidegger says, human reality. What is meant here by saying that existence precedes essence? It means that, first of all, man exists, turns up, appears on the scene, and, only afterwards, defines himself. If man, as the existentialist conceives him, is indefinable, it is because at first he is nothing. Only afterward will he be something, and he himself will have made what he will be. Thus, there is no human nature, since there is no God to conceive it. Not only is man what he conceives himself to be, but he is also only what he wills himself to be after this thrust toward existence.

Man is nothing else but what he makes of himself. Such is the first principle of existentialism. It is also what is called subjectivity, the name we are labeled with when charges are brought against us. But what do we mean by this, if not that man has a greater dignity than a stone or table? For we mean that man first exists, that is, that man first of all is the being who hurls himself toward a future and who is conscious of imagining himself as being in the future. Man is at the start a plan which is aware of itself, rather than a patch of moss, a piece of garbage, or a cauliflower; nothing exists prior to this plan; there is nothing in heaven; man will be what he will have planned to be. Not what he will want to be. Because by the word "will" we generally mean a conscious decision, which is subsequent to what we have already made of ourselves. I may want to belong to a political party, write a book, get married; but all that is only a manifestation of an earlier, more spontaneous choice that is called "will." But if existence really does precede essence, man is responsible for what he is. Thus, existentialism's first move is to make every man aware of what he is and to make the full responsibility of his existence rest on him. And when we say that a man is responsible for himself, we do not only mean that he is responsible for his own individuality, but that he is responsible for all men.

The word subjectivism has two meanings, and our opponents play on the two. Subjectivism means, on the one hand, that an individual chooses and makes himself; and, on the other, that it is impossible for man to transcend human subjectivity. The second of these is the essential meaning of existentialism. When we say that man chooses his own self, we mean that every one of us does likewise; but we also mean by that that in making this choice he also chooses all men. In fact, in creating the man that we want to be, there is not a single one of our acts which does not at the same time create an image of man as we think he ought to be. To choose to be this or that is to affirm at the same time the value of what we choose, because we can never choose evil. We always choose the good, and nothing can be good for us without being good for all.

If, on the other hand, existence precedes essence, and if we grant that we exist and fashion our image at one and the same time, the image is valid for everybody and for our whole age. Thus, our responsibility is much greater than we might have supposed, because it involves all mankind. If I am a workingman and choose to join a Christian trade-union rather than be a communist, and if by being a member I want to show that the best thing for man is resignation, that the kingdom of man is not of this world, I am not only involving my own case—I want to be resigned for everyone. As a result, my action has involved all humanity. To take a more individual matter, if I want to marry, to have children; even if this marriage depends solely on my own circumstances or passion or wish, I am involving all humanity in monogamy and not merely myself. Therefore, I am responsible for myself and for everyone else. I am creating a certain image of man of my own choosing. In choosing myself, I choose man.

This helps us understand what the actual content is of such rather grandiloquent words as anguish, forlornness, despair. As you will see, it's all quite simple.

First, what is meant by anguish? The existentialists say at once that man is anguish. What that means is this: the man who involves himself and who realizes that he is not only the person he chooses to be, but also a lawmaker who is, at the same time, choosing all mankind as well as himself, can not help escape the feeling of his total and deep responsibility. Of course, there are many people who are not anxious; but we claim that they are hiding their anxiety, that they are fleeing from it. Certainly, many people believe that when they do something, they themselves are the only ones involved, and when someone says to them, "What if everyone acted that way?" they shrug their shoulders and answer, "Everyone doesn't act that way." But really, one should always ask himself, "What would hap-

pen if everybody looked at things that way?"
There is no escaping this disturbing thought
except by a kind of double-dealing. A man who
lies and makes excuses for himself by saying
"not everybody does that," is someone with an
uneasy conscience, because the act of lying
implies that a universal value is conferred
upon the lie.

Anguish is evident even when it conceals itself. This is the anguish that Kierkegaard called
the anguish of Abraham. You know the story:
an angel has ordered Abraham to sacrifice his
son; if it really were an angel who has come
and said, "You are Abraham, you shall sacrifice
your son," everything would be all right. But
everyone might first wonder, "Is it really an
angel, and am I really Abraham? What proof
do I have?"

There was a madwoman who had hallucina-
tions; someone used to speak to her on the tel-
ephone and give her orders. Her doctor asked
her, "Who is it who talks to you?" She answered, "He says it's God." What proof did she
really have that it was God? If an angel comes
to me, what proof is there that it's an angel?
And if I hear voices, what proof is there that
they come from heaven and not from hell, or
from the subconscious, or a pathological condition? What proves that they are addressed to
me? What proof is there that I have been ap-

pointed to impose my choice and my conception of man on humanity? I'll never find any proof or sign to convince me of that. If a voice addresses me, it is always for me to decide that this is the angel's voice; if I consider that such an act is a good one, it is I who will choose to say that it is good rather than bad.

Now, I'm not being singled out as an Abraham, and yet at every moment I'm obliged to perform exemplary acts. For every man, everything happens as if all mankind had its eyes fixed on him and were guiding itself by what he does. And every man ought to say to himself, "Am I really the kind of man who has the right to act in such a way that humanity might guide itself by my actions?" And if he does not say that to himself, he is masking his anguish.

There is no question here of the kind of anguish which would lead to quietism, to inaction. It is a matter of a simple sort of anguish that anybody who has had responsibilities is familiar with. For example, when a military officer takes the responsibility for an attack and sends a certain number of men to death, he chooses to do so, and in the main he alone makes the choice. Doubtless, orders come from above, but they are too broad; he interprets them, and on this interpretation depend the lives of ten or fourteen or twenty men. In making a decision he can not help having a certain anguish. All leaders know this anguish. That doesn't keep them from acting; on the contrary, it is the very condition of their action. For it implies that they envisage a number of possibilities, and when they choose one, they realize that it has value only because it is chosen. We shall see that this kind of anguish, which is the kind that existentialism describes, is explained, in addition, by a direct responsibility to the other men whom it involves. It is not a curtain separating us from action, but is part of action itself.

When we speak of forlornness, a term Heidegger was fond of, we mean only that God does not exist and that we have to face all the consequences of this. The existentialist is strongly opposed to a certain kind of secular ethics which would like to abolish God with the least possible expense. About 1880, some French teachers tried to set up a secular ethics which went something like this: God is a useless and costly hypothesis; we are discarding it; but, meanwhile, in order for there to be an ethics, a society, a civilization, it is essential that certain values be taken seriously and that they be considered as having an *a priori* existence. It must be obligatory, *a priori*, to be honest, not to lie, not to beat your wife, to have children, etc., etc. So we're going to try a little device which will make it possible to show that values exist all the same, inscribed in a heaven of ideas, though otherwise God does not exist. In other words—and this, I believe, is the tendency of everything called reformism in France—nothing will be changed if God does not exist. We shall find ourselves with the same norms of honesty, progress, and humanism, and we shall have made of God an outdated hypothesis which will peacefully die off by itself.

The existentialist, on the contrary, thinks it very distressing that God does not exist, because all possibility of finding values in a heaven of ideas disappears along with Him; there can no longer be an *a priori* Good, since there is no infinite and perfect consciousness to think it. Nowhere is it written that the Good exists, that we must be honest, that we must not lie; because the fact is we are on a plane where there are only men. Dostoievsky said, "If God didn't exist, everything would be possible." That is the very starting point of existentialism. Indeed, everything is permissible if God does not exist, and as a result man is forlorn, because neither within him nor without does he find anything to cling to. He can't start making excuses for himself.

If existence really does precede essence, there is no explaining things away by reference to a fixed and given human nature. In other words, there is no determinism, man is free, man is freedom. On the other hand, if God does not exist, we find no values or commands to turn to which legitimize our conduct. So, in the bright realm of values, we have no excuse behind us, nor justification before us. We are alone, with no excuses.

That is the idea I shall try to convey when I say that man is condemned to be free. Condemned, because he did not create himself, yet, in other respects is free; because, once thrown into the world, he is responsible for everything he does. The existentialist does not believe in the power of passion. He will never agree that a sweeping passion is a ravaging torrent which fatally leads a man to certain acts and is therefore an excuse. He thinks that man is responsible for his passion.

The existentialist does not think that man is going to help himself by finding in the world some omen by which to orient himself. Because he thinks that man will interpret the omen to suit himself. Therefore, he thinks that man, with no support and no aid, is condemned every moment to invent man. Ponge, in a very fine article, has said, "Man is the future of man." That's exactly it. But if it is taken to mean that this future is recorded in heaven, that God sees it, then it is false, because it would really no longer be a future. If it is taken to mean that, whatever a man may be, there is a future to be forged, a virgin future before him, then this remark is sound. But then we are forlorn.

To give you an example which will enable you to understand forlornness better, I shall cite the case of one of my students who came to see me under the following circumstances: his father was on bad terms with his mother, and, moreover, was inclined to be a collaborationist; his older brother had been killed in the German offensive of 1940, and the young man, with somewhat immature but generous feelings, wanted to avenge him. His mother lived alone with him, very much upset by the half-treason of her husband and the death of her older son; the boy was her only consolation.

The boy was faced with the choice of leaving for England and joining the Free French Forces—that is, leaving his mother behind— or remaining with his mother and helping her to carry on. He was fully aware that the woman lived only for him and that his going-off—and perhaps his death—would plunge her into despair. He was also aware that every act that he did for his mother's sake was a sure thing, in the sense that it was helping her to carry on, whereas every effort he made toward going off and fighting was an uncertain move which might run aground and prove completely useless; for example, on his way to England he might, while passing through Spain, be detained indefinitely in a Spanish camp; he might reach England or Algiers and be stuck in an office at a desk job. As a result, he was faced with two very different kinds of action: one, concrete, immediate, but concerning only one individual; the other concerned an incomparably vaster group, a national collectivity, but for that very reason was dubious, and might be interrupted en route. And, at the same time, he was wavering between two kinds of ethics. On the one hand, an ethics of sympathy, of personal devotion; on the other, a broader ethics, but one whose efficacy was more dubious. He had to choose between the two.

Who could help him choose? Christian doctrine? No. Christian doctrine says, "Be charitable, love your neighbor, take the more rugged path, etc., etc." But which is the more rugged path? Whom should he love as a brother? The fighting man or his mother? Which does the greater good, the vague act of fighting in a group, or the concrete one of helping a particular human being to go on living? Who can decide *a priori?* Nobody. No book of ethics can tell him. The Kantian ethics says, "Never treat any person as a means, but as an end." Very well, if I stay with my mother, I'll treat her as an end and not as a means; but by virtue of this very fact, I'm running the risk of treating the people around me who are fighting, as means; and, conversely, if I go to join those who are fighting, I'll be treating them as an end, and, by doing that, I run the risk of treating my mother as a means.

If values are vague, and if they are always too broad for the concrete and specific case that we are considering, the only thing left for us is to trust our instincts. That's what this young man tried to do; and when I saw him, he said, "In the end, feeling is what counts. I ought to choose whichever pushes me in one direction. If I feel that I love my mother enough to sacrifice everything else for her— my desire for vengeance, for action, for adventure—then I'll stay with her. If, on the contrary, I feel that my love for my mother isn't enough, I'll leave."

But how is the value of a feeling determined? What gives his feeling for his mother value? Precisely the fact that he remained with her. I may say that I like so-and-so well enough to sacrifice a certain amount of money for him, but I may say so only if I've done it. I may say "I love my mother well enough to remain with her" if I have remained with her.

The only way to determine the value of this affection is, precisely, to perform an act which confirms and defines it. But, since I require this affection to justify my act, I find myself caught in a vicious circle.

On the other hand, Gide has well said that a mock feeling and a true feeling are almost indistinguishable; to decide that I love my mother and will remain with her, or to remain with her by putting on an act, amount somewhat to the same thing. In other words, the feeling is formed by the acts one performs; so, I can not refer to it in order to act upon it. Which means that I can neither seek within myself the true condition which will impel me to act, nor apply to a system of ethics for concepts which will permit me to act. You will say, "At least, he did go to a teacher for advice." But if you seek advice from a priest, for example, you have chosen this priest; you already knew, more or less, just about what advice he was going to give you. In other words, choosing your adviser is involving yourself. The proof of this is that if you are a Christian, you will say, "Consult a priest." But some priests are collaborating, some are just marking time, some are resisting. Which to choose? If the young man chooses a priest who is resisting or collaborating, he has already decided on the kind of advice he's going to get. Therefore, in coming to see me he knew the answer I was going to give him, and I had only one answer to give: "You're free, choose, that is, invent." No general ethics can show you what is to be done; there are no omens in the world. The Catholics will reply, "But there are." Granted—but, in any case, I myself choose the meaning they have.

When I was a prisoner, I knew a rather remarkable young man who was a Jesuit. He had entered the Jesuit order in the following way: he had had a number of very bad breaks; in childhood, his father died, leaving him in poverty, and he was a scholarship student at a religious institution where he was constantly made to feel that he was being kept out of charity; then, he failed to get any of the honors and distinctions that children like; later on, at about eighteen, he bungled a love affair; finally, at twenty-two, he failed in military training, a childish enough matter, but it was the last straw.

This young fellow might well have felt that he had botched everything. It was a sign of something, but of what? He might have taken refuge in bitterness or despair. But he very wisely looked upon all this as a sign that he was not made for secular triumphs, and that only the triumphs of religion, holiness, and faith were open to him. He saw the hand of

God in all this, and so he entered the order.
Who can help seeing that he alone decided
what the sign meant?

Some other interpretation might have been
drawn from this series of setbacks; for example, that he might have done better to turn
carpenter or revolutionist. Therefore, he is
fully responsible for the interpretation. Forlornness implies that we ourselves choose our
being. Forlornness and anguish go together.

As for despair, the term has a very simple
meaning. It means that we shall confine ourselves to reckoning only with what depends
upon our will, or on the ensemble of probabilities which make our action possible. When we
want something, we always have to reckon with
probabilities. I may be counting on the ar-
rival of a friend. The friend is coming by rail
or street-car; this supposes that the train will
arrive on schedule, or that the street-car will
not jump the track. I am left in the realm of
possibility; but possibilities are to be reck-
oned with only to the point where my action
comports with the ensemble of these possibilities, and no further. The moment the possibilities I am considering are not rigorously
involved by my action, I ought to disengage
myself from them, because no God, no scheme,
can adapt the world and its possibilities to my
will. When Descartes said, "Conquer your-

self rather than the world," he meant essentially the same thing.

The Marxists to whom I have spoken reply, "You can rely on the support of others in your action, which obviously has certain limits because you're not going to live forever. That means: rely on both what others are doing elsewhere to help you, in China, in Russia, and what they will do later on, after your death, to carry on the action and lead it to its fulfillment, which will be the revolution. You even *have* to rely upon that, otherwise you're immoral." I reply at once that I will always rely on fellow-fighters insofar as these comrades are involved with me in a common struggle, in the unity of a party or a group in which I can more or less make my weight felt; that is, one whose ranks I am in as a fighter and whose movements I am aware of at every moment. In such a situation, relying on the unity and will of the party is exactly like counting on the fact that the train will arrive on time or that the car won't jump the track. But, given that man is free and that there is no human nature for me to depend on, I can not count on men whom I do not know by relying on human goodness or man's concern for the good of society. I don't know what will become of the Russian revolution; I may make an example of it to the extent that at the present time it is apparent that the proletariat plays a part in Russia that it plays in no other nation. But I can't swear that this will inevitably lead to a triumph of the proletariat. I've got to limit myself to what I see.

Given that men are free and that tomorrow they will freely decide what man will be, I can not be sure that, after my death, fellow-fighters will carry on my work to bring it to its maximum perfection. Tomorrow, after my death, some men may decide to set up Fascism, and the others may be cowardly and muddled enough to let them do it. Fascism will then be the human reality, so much the worse for us.

Actually, things will be as man will have decided they are to be. Does that mean that I should abandon myself to quietism? No. First, I should involve myself; then, act on the old saw, "Nothing ventured, nothing gained." Nor does it mean that I shouldn't belong to a party, but rather that I shall have no illusions and shall do what I can. For example, suppose I ask myself, "Will socialization, as such, ever come about?" I know nothing about it. All I know is that I'm going to do everything in my power to bring it about. Beyond that, I can't count on anything. Quietism is the attitude of people who say, "Let others do what I can't do." The doctrine I am presenting is the very opposite of quietism, since it declares, "There is no reality except in action." Moreover, it goes further, since it adds, "Man is nothing else than his plan; he exists only to the extent that he fulfills himself; he is therefore nothing else than the ensemble of his acts, nothing else than his life."

According to this, we can understand why our doctrine horrifies certain people. Because often the only way they can bear their wretchedness is to think, "Circumstances have been against me. What I've been and done doesn't show my true worth. To be sure, I've had no great love, no great friendship, but that's because I haven't met a man or woman who was worthy. The books I've written haven't been very good because I haven't had the proper leisure. I haven't had children to devote myself to because I didn't find a man with whom I could have spent my life. So there remains within me, unused and quite viable, a host of propensities, inclinations, possibilities, that one wouldn't guess from the mere series of things I've done."

Now, for the existentialist there is really no love other than one which manifests itself in a person's being in love. There is no genius other than one which is expressed in works of art; the genius of Proust is the sum of Proust's works; the genius of Racine is his series of tragedies. Outside of that, there is nothing. Why say that Racine could have written another tragedy, when he didn't write it? A man is involved in life, leaves his impress on it, and outside of that there is nothing. To be sure, this may seem a harsh thought to someone whose life hasn't been a success. But, on the other hand, it prompts people to understand that reality alone is what counts, that dreams, expectations, and hopes warrant no more than to define a man as a disappointed dream, as miscarried hopes, as vain expectations. In other words, to define him negatively and not positively. However, when we say, "You are nothing else than your life," that does not imply that the artist will be judged solely on the basis of his works of art; a thousand other things will contribute toward summing him up. What we mean is that a man is nothing else than a series of undertakings, that he is the sum, the organization, the ensemble of the relationships which make up these undertakings.

When all is said and done, what we are accused of, at bottom, is not our pessimism, but an optimistic toughness. If people throw up to us our works of fiction in which we write about people who are soft, weak, cowardly, and

sometimes even downright bad, it's not because these people are soft, weak, cowardly, or
bad; because if we were to say, as Zola did,
that they are that way because of heredity, the
workings of environment, society, because of
biological or psychological determinism, people would be reassured. They would say,
"Well, that's what we're like, no one can do
anything about it." But when the existentialist writes about a coward, he says that this coward is responsible for his cowardice. He's not
like that because he has a cowardly heart or
lung or brain; he's not like that on account of
his physiological make-up; but he's like that
because he has made himself a coward by his
acts. There's no such thing as a cowardly constitution; there are nervous constitutions;
there is poor blood, as the common people
say, or strong constitutions. But the man whose
blood is poor is not a coward on that account,
for what makes cowardice is the act of renouncing or yielding. A constitution is not an act;
the coward is defined on the basis of the acts
he performs. People feel, in a vague sort of
way, that this coward we're talking about is
guilty of being a coward, and the thought
frightens them, What people would like is that
a coward or a hero be born that way.

One of the complaints most frequently

made about *The Ways of Freedom** can be summed up as follows: "After all, these people are so spineless, how are you going to make heroes out of them?" This objection almost makes me laugh, for it assumes that people are born heroes. That's what people really want to think. If you're born cowardly, you may set your mind perfectly at rest; there's nothing you can do about it; you'll be cowardly all your life, whatever you may do. If you're born a hero, you may set your mind just as much at rest; you'll be a hero all your life; you'll drink like a hero and eat like a hero. What the existentialist says is that the coward makes himself cowardly, that the hero makes himself heroic. There's always a possibility for the coward not to be cowardly any more and for the hero to stop being heroic. What counts is total involvement; some one particular action or set of circumstances is not total involvement.

Thus, I think we have answered a number of the charges concerning existentialism. You see that it can not be taken for a philosophy of quietism, since it defines man in terms of action; nor for a pessimistic description of man— there is no doctrine more optimistic, since

* *Les Chemins de la Liberté*, M. Sartre's projected trilogy of novels, two of which, *L'Age de Raison* (*The Age of Reason*) and *Le Sursis* (*The Reprieve*) have already appeared.—Translator's note.

man's destiny is within himself; nor for an attempt to discourage man from acting, since it tells him that the only hope is in his acting and that action is the only thing that enables a man to live. Consequently, we are dealing here with an ethics of action and involvement.

Nevertheless, on the basis of a few notions like these, we are still charged with immuring man in his private subjectivity. There again we're very much misunderstood. Subjectivity of the individual is indeed our point of departure, and this for strictly philosophic reasons. Not because we are bourgeois, but because we want a doctrine based on truth and not a lot of fine theories, full of hope but with no real basis. There can be no other truth to take off from than this: *I think; therefore, I exist.* There we have the absolute truth of consciousness becoming aware of itself. Every theory which takes man out of the moment in which he becomes aware of himself is, at its very beginning, a theory which confounds truth, for outside the Cartesian *cogito,* all views are only probable, and a doctrine of probability which is not bound to a truth dissolves into thin air. In order to describe the probable, you must have a firm hold on the true. Therefore, before there can be any truth whatsoever, there must be an absolute truth; and this one is simple and easily arrived at; it's on everyone's doorstep; it's a matter of grasping it directly.

Secondly, this theory is the only one which gives man dignity, the only one which does not reduce him to an object. The effect of all materialism is to treat all men, including the one philosophizing, as objects, that is, as an ensemble of determined reactions in no way distinguished from the ensemble of qualities and phenomena which constitute a table or a chair or a stone. We definitely wish to establish the human realm as an ensemble of values distinct from the material realm. But the subjectivity that we have thus arrived at, and which we have claimed to be truth, is not a strictly individual subjectivity, for we have demonstrated that one discovers in the *cogito* not only himself, but others as well.

The philosophies of Descartes and Kant to the contrary, through the *I think* we reach our own self in the presence of others, and the others are just as real to us as our own self. Thus, the man who becomes aware of himself through the *cogito* also perceives all others, and he perceives them as the condition of his own existence. He realizes that he can not be anything (in the sense that we say that someone is witty or nasty or jealous) unless others recognize it as such. In order to get any truth about myself, I must have contact with

another person. The other is indispensable to
my own existence, as well as to my knowledge
about myself. This being so, in discovering my
inner being I discover the other person at the
same time, like a freedom placed in front of
me which thinks and wills only for or against
me. Hence, let us at once announce the discovery of a world which we shall call inter-
subjectivity; this is the world in which man
decides what he is and what others are.

Besides, if it is impossible to find in every
man some universal essence which would be
human nature, yet there does exist a universal
human condition. It's not by chance that today's thinkers speak more readily of man's condition than of his nature. By condition they
mean, more or less definitely, the *a priori*
limits which outline man's fundamental situation in the universe. Historical situations vary;
a man may be born a slave in a pagan society or
a feudal lord or a proletarian. What does not
vary is the necessity for him to exist in the
world, to be at work there, to be there in the
midst of other people, and to be mortal there.
The limits are neither subjective nor objective,
or, rather, they have an objective and a subjective side. Objective because they are to
be found everywhere and are recognizable everywhere; subjective because they are *lived*
and are nothing if man does not live them, that

is, freely determine his existence with reference to them. And though the configurations may differ, at least none of them are completely strange to me, because they all appear as attempts either to pass beyond these limits or recede from them or deny them or adapt to them. Consequently, every configuration, however individual it may be, has a universal value.

Every configuration, even the Chinese, the Indian, or the Negro, can be understood by a Westerner. "Can be understood" means that by virtue of a situation that he can imagine, a European of 1945 can, in like manner, push himself to his limits and reconstitute within himself the configuration of the Chinese, the Indian, or the African. Every configuration has universality in the sense that every configuration can be understood by every man. This does not at all mean that this configuration defines man forever, but that it can be met with again. There is always a way to understand the idiot, the child, the savage, the foreigner, provided one has the necessary information.

In this sense we may say that there is a universality of man; but it is not given, it is perpetually being made. I build the universal in choosing myself; I build it in understanding the configuration of every other man, whatever age he might have lived in. This absoluteness of choice does not do away with the relative-

ness of each epoch. At heart, what existentialism shows is the connection between the absolute character of free involvement, by virtue
of which every man realizes himself in realizing a type of mankind, an involvement always
comprehensible in any age whatsoever and by
any person whosoever, and the relativeness of
the cultural ensemble which may result from
such a choice; it must be stressed that the rela-
tivity of Cartesianism and the absolute character of Cartesian involvement go together. In
this sense, you may, if you like, say that each
of us performs an absolute act in breathing,
eating, sleeping, or behaving in any way whatever. There is no difference between being free,
like a configuration, like an existence which
chooses its essence, and being absolute. There
is no difference between being an absolute
temporarily localized, that is, localized in history, and being universally comprehensible.

This does not entirely settle the objection to
subjectivism. In fact, the objection still takes
several forms. First, there is the following: we
are told, "So you're able to do anything, no
matter what!" This is expressed in various
ways. First we are accused of anarchy; then
they say, "You're unable to pass judgment on
others, because there's no reason to prefer one
configuration to another"; finally they tell us,
"Everything is arbitrary in this choosing of

yours. You take something from one pocket
and pretend you're putting it into the other."

These three objections aren't very serious.
Take the first objection. "You're able to do anything, no matter what" is not to the point. In
one sense choice is possible, but what is not
possible is not to choose. I can always choose,
but I ought to know that if I do not choose, I
am still choosing. Though this may seem purely
formal, it is highly important for keeping fan-
tasy and caprice within bounds. If it is true
that in facing a situation, for example, one in
which, as a person capable of having sexual relations, of having children, I am obliged to
choose an attitude, and if I in any way assume
responsibility for a choice which, in involving
myself, also involves all mankind, this has nothing to do with caprice, even if no *a priori* value
determines my choice.

If anybody thinks that he recognizes here
Gide's theory of the arbitrary act, he fails to
see the enormous difference between this doctrine and Gide's. Gide does not know what a
situation is. He acts out of pure caprice. For
us, on the contrary, man is in an organized situation in which he himself is involved.
Through his choice, he involves all mankind,
and he can not avoid making a choice: either
he will remain chaste, or he will marry without having children, or he will marry and have

children; anyhow, whatever he may do, it is impossible for him not to take full responsibility for the way he handles this problem. Doubtless, he chooses without referring to pre-established values, but it is unfair to accuse him of caprice. Instead, let us say that moral choice is to be compared to the making of a work of art. And before going any further, let it be said at once that we are not dealing here with an aesthetic ethics, because our opponents are so dishonest that they even accuse us of that. The example I've chosen is a comparison only.

Having said that, may I ask whether anyone has ever accused an artist who has painted a picture of not having drawn his inspiration from rules set up *a priori?* Has anyone ever asked, "What painting ought he to make?" It is clearly understood that there is no definite painting to be made, that the artist is engaged in the making of his painting, and that the painting to be made is precisely the painting he will have made. It is clearly understood that there are no *a priori* aesthetic values, but that there are values which appear subsequently in the coherence of the painting, in the correspondence between what the artist intended and the result. Nobody can tell what the painting of tomorrow will be like. Painting can be judged only after it has once been made. What connection does that have with ethics? We are in the same creative situation. We never say that a work of art is arbitrary. When we speak of a canvas of Picasso, we never say that it is arbitrary; we understand quite well that he was making himself what he is at the very time he was painting, that the ensemble of his work is embodied in his life.

The same holds on the ethical plane. What art and ethics have in common is that we have creation and invention in both cases. We can not decide *a priori* what there is to be done. I think that I pointed that out quite sufficiently when I mentioned the case of the student who came to see me, and who might have applied to all the ethical systems, Kantian or other-wise, without getting any sort of guidance. He was obliged to devise his law himself. Never let it be said by us that this man—who, taking affection, individual action, and kind-hearted-ness toward a specific person as his ethical first principle, chooses to remain with his mother, or who, preferring to make a sacrifice, chooses to go to England—has made an arbitrary choice. Man makes himself. He isn't ready made at the start. In choosing his ethics, he makes himself, and force of circumstances is such that he can not abstain from choosing one.

We define man only in relationship to involvement. It is therefore absurd to charge us with arbitrariness of choice.

In the second place, it is said that we are unable to pass judgment on others. In a way this is true, and in another way, false. It is true in this sense, that, whenever a man sanely and sincerely involves himself and chooses his configuration, it is impossible for him to prefer another configuration, regardless of what his own may be in other respects. It is true in this sense, that we do not believe in progress. Progress is betterment. Man is always the same. The situation confronting him varies. Choice always remains a choice in a situation. The problem has not changed since the time one could choose between those for and those against slavery, for example, at the time of the Civil War, and the present time, when one can side with the Maquis Resistance Party, or with the Communists.

But, nevertheless, one can still pass judgment, for, as I have said, one makes a choice in relationship to others. First, one can judge (and this is perhaps not a judgment of value, but a logical judgment) that certain choices are based on error and others on truth. If we have defined man's situation as a free choice, with no excuses and no recourse, every man who takes refuge behind the excuse of his passions, every man who sets up a determinism, is a dishonest man.

The objection may be raised, "But why mayn't he choose himself dishonestly?" I reply that I am not obliged to pass moral judgment on him, but that I do define his dishonesty as an error. One can not help considering the truth of the matter. Dishonesty is obviously a falsehood because it belies the complete freedom of involvement. On the same grounds, I maintain that there is also dishonesty if I choose to state that certain values exist prior to me; it is self-contradictory for me to want them and at the same state that they are imposed on me. Suppose someone says to me, "What if I want to be dishonest?" I'll answer, "There's no reason for you not to be, but I'm saying that that's what you are, and that the strictly coherent attitude is that of honesty."

Besides, I can bring moral judgment to bear. When I declare that freedom in every concrete circumstance can have no other aim than to want itself, if man has once become aware that in his forlornness he imposes values, he can no longer want but one thing, and that is freedom, as the basis of all values. That doesn't mean that he wants it in the abstract. It means simply that the ultimate meaning of the acts of honest men is the quest for freedom as such. A man who belongs to a communist or revolutionary union wants concrete goals; these goals imply an abstract desire for freedom; but this freedom is wanted in something concrete. We want freedom for freedom's sake and in every particular circumstance. And in wanting freedom we discover that it depends entirely on the freedom of others, and that the freedom of others depends on ours. Of course, freedom as the definition of man does not depend on others, but as soon as there is involvement, I am obliged to want others to have freedom at the same time that I want my own freedom. I can take freedom as my goal only if I take that of others as a goal as well. Consequently, when, in all honesty, I've recognized that man is a being in whom existence precedes essence, that he is a free being who, in various circumstances, can want only his freedom, I have at the same time recognized that I can want only the freedom of others.

Therefore, in the name of this will for freedom, which freedom itself implies, I may pass judgment on those who seek to hide from themselves the complete arbitrariness and the complete freedom of their existence. Those who hide their complete freedom from themselves out of a spirit of seriousness or by means of deterministic excuses, I shall call cowards; those who try to show that their existence was necessary, when it is the very contingency of man's appearance on earth, I shall call stinkers.

But cowards or stinkers can be judged only from a strictly unbiased point of view.

Therefore though the content of ethics is variable, a certain form of it is universal. Kant says that freedom desires both itself and the freedom of others. Granted. But he believes that the formal and the universal are enough to constitute an ethics. We, on the other hand, think that principles which are too abstract run aground in trying to decide action. Once again, take the case of the student. In the name of what, in the name of what great moral maxim do you think he could have decided, in perfect peace of mind, to abandon his mother or to stay with her? There is no way of judging. The content is always concrete and thereby unforeseeable; there is always the element of invention. The one thing that counts is knowing whether the inventing that has been done, has been done in the name of freedom.

For example, let us look at the following two cases. You will see to what extent they correspond, yet differ. Take *The Mill on the Floss*. We find a certain young girl, Maggie Tulliver, who is an embodiment of the value of passion and who is aware of it. She is in love with a young man, Stephen, who is engaged to an insignificant young girl. This Maggie Tulliver, instead of heedlessly preferring her own happiness, chooses, in the name of human solidarity, to sacrifice herself and give up the man she loves. On the other hand, Sanseverina, in *The Charterhouse of Parma*, believing that passion is man's true value, would say that a great love deserves sacrifices; that it is to be preferred to the banality of the conjugal love that would tie Stephen to the young ninny he had to marry. She would choose to sacrifice the girl and fulfill her happiness; and, as Stendhal shows, she is even ready to sacrifice herself for the sake of passion, if this life demands it. Here we are in the presence of two strictly opposed moralities. I claim that they are much the same thing; in both cases what has been set up as the goal is freedom.

You can imagine two highly similar attitudes: one girl prefers to renounce her love out of resignation; another prefers to disregard the prior attachment of the man she loves out of sexual desire. On the surface these two actions resemble those we've just described. However, they are completely different. Sanseverina's attitude is much nearer that of Maggie Tulliver, one of heedless rapacity.

Thus, you see that the second charge is true and, at the same time, false. One may choose anything if it is on the grounds of free involvement.

The third objection is the following: "You take something from one pocket and put it into the other. That is, fundamentally, values aren't serious, since you choose them." My answer to this is that I'm quite vexed that that's the way it is; but if I've discarded God the Father, there has to be someone to invent values. You've got to take things as they are. Moreover, to say that we invent values means nothing else but this: life has no meaning *a priori.* Before you come alive, life is nothing; it's up to you to give it a meaning, and value is nothing else but the meaning that you choose. In that way, you see, there is a possibility of creating a human community.

I've been reproached for asking whether existentialism is humanistic. It's been said, "But you said in *Nausea* that the humanists were all wrong. You made fun of a certain kind of humanist. Why come back to it now?" Actually, the word humanism has two very different meanings. By humanism one can mean a theory which takes man as an end and as a higher value. Humanism in this sense can be found in Cocteau's tale *Around the World in Eighty Hours* when a character, because he is flying over some mountains in an airplane, declares, "Man is simply amazing." That means that I, who did not build the airplanes, shall personally benefit from these particular inventions, and that I, as man, shall personally consider myself responsible for, and honored by, acts of a few particular men. This would imply that we ascribe a value to man on the basis of the highest deeds of certain men. This humanism is absurd, because only the dog or the horse would be able to make such an over-all judgment about man, which they are careful not to do, at least to my knowledge.

But it can not be granted that a man may make a judgment about man. Existentialism spares him from any such judgment. The existentialist will never consider man as an end because he is always in the making. Nor should we believe that there is a mankind to which we might set up a cult in the manner of Auguste Comte. The cult of mankind ends in the self-enclosed humanism of Comte, and, let it be said, of fascism. This kind of humanism we can do without.

But there is another meaning of humanism. Fundamentally it is this: man is constantly outside of himself; in projecting himself, in losing himself outside of himself, he makes for man's existing; and, on the other hand, it is by pursuing transcendent goals that he is able to exist; man, being this state of passing-beyond, and seizing upon things only as they bear upon this passing-beyond, is at the heart, at the center of this passing-beyond. There is no universe other than a human universe, the universe of human subjectivity. This connection between transcendency, as a constituent element of man —not in the sense that God is transcendent, but in the sense of passing beyond—and subjectivity, in the sense that man is not closed in on himself but is always present in a human universe, is what we call existentialism human- ism. Humanism, because we remind man that there is no law-maker other than himself, and that in his forlornness he will decide by him- self; because we point out that man will fulfill himself as man, not in turning toward himself, but in seeking outside of himself a goal which is just this liberation, just this particular ful- fillment.

From these few reflections it is evident that nothing is more unjust than the objections that have been raised against us. Existentialism is nothing else than an attempt to draw all the consequences of a coherent atheistic position. It isn't trying to plunge man into despair at all. But if one calls every attitude of unbelief despair, like the Christians, then the word is not being used in its original sense. Existential- ism isn't so atheistic that it wears itself out showing that God doesn't exist. Rather, it de- clares that even if God did exist, that would change nothing. There you've got our point of view. Not that we believe that God exists, but we think that the problem of His existence is not the issue. In this sense existentialism is op- timistic, a doctrine of action, and it is plain dis- honesty for Christians to make no distinction between their own despair and ours and then to call us despairing.

FREEDOM AND RESPONSIBILITY

ALTHOUGH the considerations which are about to follow are of interest primarily to the ethicist, it may nevertheless be worthwhile after these descriptions and arguments to return to the freedom of the for-itself and to try to understand what the fact of this freedom represents for human destiny.

The essential consequence of our earlier remarks is that man being condemned to be free carries the weight of the whole world on his shoulders; he is responsible for the world and for himself as a way of being. We are taking the word "responsibility" in its ordinary sense as "consciousness (of) being the incontestable author of an event or of an object." In this sense the responsibility of the for-itself is overwhelming since he* is the one by whom it happens that *there is* a world; since he is also the one who makes himself be, then whatever may be the situation in which he finds himself, the for-itself must wholly assume this situation with its peculiar coefficient of ad-

* I am shifting to the personal pronoun here since Sartre is describing the for-itself in concrete personal terms rather than as a metaphysical entity. Strictly speaking, of course, this is his position throughout, and the French "*il*" is indifferently "he" or "it." Tr.

versity, even though it be insupportable. He must assume the situation with the proud consciousness of being the author of it, for the very worst disadvantages or the worst threats which can endanger my person have meaning only in and through my project; and it is on the ground of the engagement which I am that they appear. It is therefore senseless to think of complaining since nothing foreign has decided what we feel, what we live, or what we are.

Furthermore this absolute responsibility is not resignation; it is simply the logical requirement of the consequences of our freedom. What happens to me happens through me, and I can neither affect myself with it nor revolt against it nor resign myself to it. Moreover everything which happens to me is *mine*. By this we must understand first of all that I am always equal to what happens to me *qua* man, for what happens to a man through other men and through himself can be only human. The most terrible situations of war, the worst tortures do not create a non-human state of things; there is no non-human situation. It is only through fear, flight, and recourse to magical types of conduct that I shall decide on the non-human, but this decision is human, and I shall carry the entire responsibility for it. But in addition the situation is *mine* because it is the image of my free choice of myself, and everything which it presents to me is *mine* in that this represents me and symbolizes me. Is it not I who decide the coefficient of adversity in things and even their unpredictability by deciding myself?

Thus there are no *accidents* in a life; a community event which suddenly bursts forth and involves me in it does not come from the outside. If I am mobilized in a war, this war is *my* war; it is in my image and I deserve it. I deserve it first because I could always get out of it by suicide or by desertion; these ultimate possibles are those which must always be present for us when there is a question of envisaging a situation. For lack of getting out of it, I have *chosen* it. This can be due to inertia, to cowardice in the face of public opinion, or because I prefer certain other values to the value of the refusal to join in the war (the good opinion of my relatives, the honor of my family, *etc.*). Anyway you look at it, it is a matter of a choice. This choice will be repeated later on again and again without a break until the end of the war. Therefore we must agree with the statement by J. Romains, "In war there are no innocent victims." * If therefore I have preferred war to death or to dishonor,

* J. Romains: *Les hommes de bonne volonté;* "Prélude à Verdun."

everything takes place as if I bore the entire responsibility for this war. Of course others have declared it, and one might be tempted perhaps to consider me as a simple accomplice. But this notion of complicity has only a juridical sense, and it does not hold here. For it depended on me that for me and by me this war should not exist, and I have decided that it does exist. There was no compulsion here, for the compulsion could have got no hold on a freedom. I did not have any excuse; for as we have said repeatedly in this book, the peculiar character of human-reality is that it is without excuse. Therefore it remains for me only to lay claim to this war.

But in addition the war is *mine* because by the sole fact that it arises in a situation which I cause to be and that I can discover it there only by engaging myself for or against it, I can no longer distinguish at present the choice which I make of myself from the choice which I make of the war. To live this war is to choose myself through it and to choose it through my choice of myself. There can be no question of considering it as "four years of vacation" or as a "reprieve," as a "recess," the essential part of my responsibilities being elsewhere in my married, family, or professional life. In this war which I have chosen I choose myself from day to day, and I make it mine by making myself. If it is going to be four empty years, then it is I who bear the responsibility for this.

Finally, as we pointed out earlier, each person is an absolute choice of self from the standpoint of a world of knowledges and of techniques which this choice both assumes and illumines; each person is an absolute upsurge at an absolute date and is perfectly unthinkable at another date. It is therefore a waste of time to ask what I should have been if this war had not broken out, for I have chosen myself as one of the possible meanings of the epoch which imperceptibly led to war. I am not distinct from this same epoch; I could not be transported to another epoch without contradiction. Thus *I am* this war which restricts and limits and makes comprehensible the period which preceded it. In this sense we may define more precisely the responsibility of the for-itself if to the earlier quoted statement, "There are no innocent victims," we add the words, "We have the war we deserve." Thus, totally free, undistinguishable from the period for which I have chosen to be the meaning, as profoundly responsible for the war as if I had myself declared it, unable to live without integrating it in *my* situation, engaging myself in it wholly and stamping it with my seal, I must be without remorse or regrets as I am without excuse; for from the instant of my upsurge into being, I carry the weight of the world by myself alone without anything or any person being able to lighten it.

Yet this responsibility is of a very particular type. Someone will say, "I did not ask to be born." This is a naive way of throwing greater emphasis on our facticity. I am responsible for everything, in fact, except for my very responsibility, for I am not the foundation of my being. Therefore everything takes place as if I were compelled to be responsible. I am *abandoned* in the world, not in the sense that I might remain abandoned and passive in a hostile universe like a board floating on the water, but rather in the sense that I find myself suddenly alone and without help, engaged in a world for which I bear the whole responsibility without being able, whatever I do, to tear myself away from this responsibility for an instant. For I am responsible for my very desire of fleeing responsibilities. To make myself passive in the world, to refuse to act upon things and upon Others is still to choose myself, and suicide is one mode among others of being-in-the-world. Yet I find an absolute responsibility for the fact that my facticity (here the fact of my birth) is directly inapprehensible and even inconceivable, for this fact of my birth never appears as a brute fact but always across a projective reconstruction of my for-itself. I am ashamed of being born or

I am astonished at it or I rejoice over it, or in attempting to get rid of my life I affirm that I live and I assume this life as bad. Thus in a certain sense I *choose* being born. This choice itself is integrally affected with facticity since I am not able not to choose, but this facticity in turn will appear only in so far as I surpass it toward my ends. Thus facticity is everywhere but inapprehensible; I never encounter anything except my responsibility. That is why I can not ask, "*Why* was I born?" or curse the day of my birth or declare that I did not ask to be born, for these various attitudes toward my birth—*i.e.*, toward the *fact* that I realize a presence in the world—are absolutely nothing else but ways of assuming this birth in full responsibility and of making it *mine*. Here again I encounter only myself and my projects so that finally my abandonment—*i.e.*, my facticity—consists simply in the fact that I am condemned to be wholly responsible for myself. I am the being which *is* in such a way that in its being its being is in question. And this "is" of my being *is* as present and inapprehensible.

Under these conditions since every event in the world can be revealed to me only as an *opportunity* (an opportunity made use of, lacked, neglected, *etc.*), or better yet since everything which happens to us can be considered as a *chance* (*i.e.,* can appear to us only as a way of realizing this being which is in question in our being) and since others as transcendences-transcended are themselves only *opportunities* and *chances,* the responsibility of the for-itself extends to the entire world as a peopled-world. It is precisely thus that the for-itself apprehends itself in anguish; that is, as a being which is neither the foundation of its own being nor of the Other's being nor of the in-itselfs which form the world, but a being which is compelled to decide the meaning of being—within it and everywhere outside of it. The one who realizes in anguish his condition as *being* thrown into a responsibility which extends to his very abandonment has no longer either remorse or regret or excuse; he is no longer anything but a freedom which perfectly reveals itself and whose being resides in this very revelation. But as we pointed out at the beginning of this work, most of the time we flee anguish in bad faith.

THE DESIRE TO BE GOD

THE MOST DISCERNING ETHICISTS have shown how a desire reaches beyond itself. Pascal believed that he could discover in hunting, for example, or tennis, or in a hundred other occupations, the need of being diverted. He revealed that in an activity which would be absurd if reduced to itself, there was a meaning which transcended it; that is, an indication which referred to the reality of man in general and to his condition. Similarly Stendhal in spite of his attachment to ideologists, and Proust in spite of his intellectualistic and analytical tendencies, have shown that love and jealousy can not be reduced to the strict desire of possessing a *particular* woman, but that these emotions aim at laying hold of the world in its entirety through the woman. This is the meaning of Stendhal's crystallization, and it is precisely for this reason that Love as Stendhal describes it appears as a mode of being in the world. Love is a fundamental relation of the for-itself to the world and to itself (selfness) through a particular woman; the woman represents only a conducting body which is placed in the circuit. These analyses may be inexact or only partially true; nevertheless they make us suspect a method other than pure analytical description. In the same way Catholic novelists immediately see in carnal love its surpassing toward God—in Don Juan, "the eternally unsatisfied," in sin, "the place empty of God." There is no question here of finding again an abstract behind the concrete; the impulse toward God is no *less concrete* than the impulse toward a particular woman. On the contrary, it is a matter of rediscovering under the partial and incomplete aspects of the subject the veritable concreteness which can be only the totality of his impulse toward being, his original relation to himself, to the world, and to the Other, in the unity of internal relations and of a fundamental project. This impulse can be only purely individual and unique. Far from estranging us from the person, as Bourget's analysis, for example, does in constituting the individual by means of a summation of general maxims, this impulse will not lead us to find in the need of writing—and of writing particular books—the need of activity in general. On the contrary, rejecting equally the theory of malleable clay and that of the bundle of drives, we will discover the individual person in the initial project which constitutes him. It is for this reason that the irreducibility of the result attained will be revealed as self-evident, not because it is the poorest and the most abstract but because it is the richest. The intuition here will be accompanied by an individual fullness.

THE BEST WAY to conceive of the fundamental
project of human reality is to say that man is the
being whose project is to be God. Whatever may
be the myths and rites of the religion considered,
God is first "sensible to the heart" of man as the
one who identifies and defines him in his ultimate and fundamental project. If man possesses
a pre-ontological comprehension of the being
of God, it is not the great wonders of nature nor
the power of society which have conferred it
upon him. God, value and supreme end of transcendence, represents the permanent limit in
terms of which man makes known to himself
what he is. To be man means to reach toward
being God. Or if you prefer, man fundamentally
is the desire to be God.

It may be asked, if man on coming into the
world is borne toward God as toward his limit,
if he can choose only to be God, what becomes
of freedom? For freedom is nothing other than
a choice which creates for itself its own possibilities, but it appears here that the initial
project of being God, which "defines" man,
comes close to being the same as a human "nature" or an "essence." The answer is that while

the *meaning* of the desire is ultimately the project of being God, the desire is never *constituted* by this meaning; on the contrary, it always represents a particular discovery of its ends. These ends in fact are pursued in terms of a particular empirical situation, and it is this very pursuit which constitutes the surroundings *as a situation*. The desire of being is always realized as the desire of a mode of being. And this desire of a mode of being expresses itself in turn as the meaning of the myriads of concrete desires which constitute the web of our conscious life. Thus we find ourselves before very complex symbolic structures which have *at least* three stories. In empirical desire I can discern a symbolization of a fundamental concrete desire which is the person himself and which represents the mode in which he has decided that being would be in question in his being. This fundamental desire in turn expresses concretely in the world within the particular situation enveloping the individual, an abstract meaningful structure which is the desire of being in general; it must be considered as human reality in the person, and it brings about his community with others, thus making it possible to state that there is a truth concerning man and not only concerning individuals who cannot be compared. Absolute concreteness, completion, existence as a totality belong then to the free

and fundamental desire which is the unique
person. Empirical desire is only a symbolization of this; it refers to this and derives its
meaning from it while remaining partial and
reducible, for the empirical desire can not be
conceived in isolation. On the other hand, the
desire of being in its abstract purity is the
truth of the concrete fundamental desire, but
it does not exist by virtue of reality. Thus
the fundamental project, the person, the free
realization of human truth is everywhere in
all desires (save for those exceptions treated
in the preceding chapter, concerning, for example, "indifferents"). It is never apprehended except through desires—as we can
apprehend space only through bodies which
shape it for us, though space is a specific reality and not a concept. Or, if you like, it is like
the *object* of Husserl, which reveals itself only
by *Abschattungen*, and which nevertheless
does not allow itself to be absorbed by any one
Abschattung. We can understand after these
remarks that the abstract, ontological "desire
to be" is unable to represent the fundamental,
human structure of the individual; it cannot
be an obstacle to his freedom. Freedom in fact,
as we have shown in the preceding chapter,
is strictly identified with nihilation. The only
being which can be called free is the being
which nihilates its being. Moreover we know

that nihilation is *lack of being* and can not be otherwise. Freedom is precisely the being which makes itself a lack of being. But since desire, as we have established, is identical with lack of being, freedom can arise only as being which makes itself a desire of being; that is, as the project-for-itself of being in-itself-for-itself. Here we have arrived at an abstract structure which can by no means be considered as the nature or essence of freedom. Freedom is existence, and in it existence precedes essence. The upsurge of freedom is immediate and concrete and is not to be distinguished from its choice; that is, from the person himself. But the structure under consideration can be called the *truth* of freedom; that is, it is the human meaning of freedom.

It should be possible to establish the human truth of the person, as we have attempted to do by an ontological phenomenology. The catalogue of empirical desires ought to be made the object of appropriate psychological investigations, observation and induction and, as needed, experience can serve to draw up this list. They will indicate to the philosopher the comprehensible relations which unite to each other various desires and various patterns of behaviors, and will bring to light certain concrete connections between the subject of experience and "situations" experientially defined (which at bottom originate only from limitations applied in the name of positivity to the fundamental situation of the subject in the world). But in establishing and classifying fundamental desires of *individual persons* neither of these methods is appropriate. Actually there can be no question of determining *a priori* and ontologically what appears in all the unpredictability of a free act. This is why we shall limit ourselves here to indicating very summarily the possibilities of such a quest and its perspectives. The very fact that we can subject any man whatsoever to such an investigation—that is what belongs to human reality in general. Or, if you prefer, this is what can be established by an ontology. But the inquiry itself and its results are on principle wholly outside the possibilities of an ontology.

EXISTENTIALIST PSYCHOANALYSIS

THE principle of this psychoanalysis is that man is a totality and not a collection. Consequently he expresses himself as a whole in even his most insignificant and his most superficial behavior. In other words there is not a taste, a mannerism, or a human act which is not *revealing*.

The *goal* of psychoanalysis is to *decipher* the empirical behavior patterns of man; that is to bring out in the open the revelations which each one of them contains and to fix them conceptually.

Its *point of departure* is *experience;* its pillar of support is the fundamental, pre-ontological comprehension which man has of the human person. Although the majority of people can well ignore the indications contained in a gesture, a word, a sign and can look with scorn on the revelation which they carry, each human individual nevertheless possesses *a priori* the *meaning* of the revelatory value of these manifestations and is capable of deciphering them, at least if he is aided and guided by a helping hand. Here as elsewhere, truth is not encountered by chance; it does not belong to a domain where one must seek it without ever having any presentiment of its location, as one can go to look for the source of the Nile or of the Niger. It belongs *a priori* to human comprehension and the essential task is an hermeneutic; that is, a deciphering, a determination, and a conceptualization.

Its *method* is comparative. Since each example of human conduct symbolizes in its own manner the fundamental choice which must be brought to light, and since at the same time each one disguises this choice under its occasional character and its historical opportunity, only the comparison of these acts of conduct can effect the emergence of the unique revelation which they all express in a different way. The first outline of this method has been furnished for us by the psychoanalysis of Freud and his disciples. For this reason it will be profitable here to indicate more specifically the points where existential psychoanalysis will be inspired by psychoanalysis proper and those where it will radically differ from it.

Both kinds of psychoanalysis consider all objectively discernible manifestations of "psychic life" as symbols maintaining symbolic relations to the fundamental, total structures which constitute the individual person. Both consider that there are no primary givens such

as hereditary dispositions, character, *etc.*
Existential psychoanalysis recognizes nothing
before the original upsurge of human freedom; empirical psychoanalysis holds that the
original affectivity of the individual is virgin
wax *before* its history. The libido is nothing
besides its concrete fixations, save for a permanent possibility of fixing anything whatsoever upon anything whatsoever. Both consider
the human being as a perpetual, searching,
historization. Rather than uncovering static,
constant givens they discover the meaning,
orientation, and adventures of this history.
Due to this fact both consider man in the
world and do not imagine that one can question the being of a man without taking into
account all his *situation.* Psychological investigations aim at reconstituting the life of the
subject from birth to the moment of the cure;
they utilize all the objective documentation
which they can find; letters, witnesses, inti-
mate diaries, "social" information of every
kind. What they aim at restoring is less a pure
psychic event than a twofold structure: the
crucial event of infancy and the psychic crystallization around this event. Here again we have
to do with a *situation.* Each "historical" fact
from this point of view will be considered at
once as a *factor* of the psychic evolution and
as a *symbol* of that evolution. For it is nothing

in itself. It operates only according to the way in which it is taken and this very manner of taking it expresses symbolically the internal disposition of the individual.

Empirical psychoanalysis and existential psychoanalysis both search within an existing situation for a fundamental attitude which can not be expressed by simple, logical definitions because it is prior to all logic, and which requires reconstruction according to the laws of specific syntheses. Empirical psychoanalysis seeks to determine the *complex,* the very name of which indicates the polyvalence of all the meanings which are referred back to it. Existential psychoanalysis seeks to determine the *original choice.* This original choice operating in the face of the world and being a choice of position in the world is total like the complex; it is prior to logic like the complex. It is this which decides the attitude of the person when confronted with logic and principles; therefore there can be no possibility of questioning it in conformance to logic. It brings together in a prelogical synthesis the totality of the existent, and as such it is the center of reference for an infinity of polyvalent meanings.

Both our psychoanalyses refuse to admit that the subject is in a privileged position to proceed in these inquiries concerning himself. They equally insist on a strictly objective method, using as documentary evidence the data of reflection as well as the testimony of others. Of course the subject *can* undertake a psychoanalytic investigation of himself. But in this case he must renounce at the outset all benefit stemming from his peculiar position and must question himself exactly as if he were someone else. Empirical psychoanalysis in fact is based on the hypothesis of the existence of an unconscious psyche, which on principle escapes the intuition of the subject. Existential psychoanalysis rejects the hypothesis of the unconscious; it makes the psychic act coextensive with consciousness. But if the fundamental project is fully experienced by the subject and hence wholly conscious, that certainly does not mean that it must by the same token be *known* by him; quite the contrary. The reader will perhaps recall the care we took in the Introduction to distinguish between consciousness and knowledge. To be sure, as we have seen earlier, reflection can be considered as a quasi-knowledge. But what it grasps at each moment is not the pure project of the for-itself as it is symbolically expressed—often in several ways at once—by the concrete behavior which it apprehends. It grasps the concrete behavior itself; that is, the specific dated desire in all its characteristic network. It grasps at once symbol and symbolization. This apprehension, to

be sure, is entirely constituted by a pre-ontological comprehension of the fundamental project; better yet, in so far as reflection is almost
a non-thetic consciousness of itself as reflection,
it *is* this same project, as well as the non-re-
flective consciousness. But it does not follow
that it commands the instruments and
techniques necessary to isolate the choice sym-
bolized, to fix it by concepts, and to bring it
forth into the full light of day. It is penetrated
by a great light without being able to express
what this light is illuminating. We are not
dealing with an unsolved riddle as the Freud-
ians believe; all is there, luminous; reflection
is in full possession of it, apprehends all. But
this "mystery in broad daylight" is due to the
fact that this possession is deprived of the
means which would ordinarily permit *analysis*
and *conceptualization*. It grasps everything, all
at once, without shading, without relief, without connections of grandeur—not that these
shades, these values, these reliefs exist some-
where and are hidden from it, but rather because they must be established by another human attitude and because they can exist only
by means of and *for* knowledge. Reflection,
unable to serve as the basis for existential
psychoanalysis, will then simply furnish us with
the brute materials toward which the psychoanalyst must take an objective attitude. Thus

only will he be able to *know* what he *already understands.* The result is that complexes uprooted from the depths of the unconscious, like projects revealed by existential psychoanalysis, will be apprehended *from the point of view of the Other.* Consequently the *object* thus brought into the light will be articulated according to the structures of the transcended-transcendence; that is, its being will be the being-for-others even if the psychoanalyst and the subject of the psychoanalysis are actually the same person. Thus the project which is brought to light by either kind of psychoanalysis can be only the totality of the individual human being, the irreducible element of the transcendence with the structure of *being-for-others.* What always escapes these methods of investigation is the project as it is for itself, the complex in its own being. This project-for-itself can be experienced only as a living possession; there is an incompatibility between existence-for-itself and objective existence. But the object of the two psychoanalyses has in it nonetheless the *reality of a being;* the subject's knowledge of it can in addition contribute to *clarify* reflection, and that reflection can then become a possession which will be a quasi-knowing.

At this point the similarity between the two kinds of psychoanalysis ceases. They differ fun-

damentally in that empirical psychoanalysis
has decided upon its own irreducible instead
of allowing this to make itself known in a
self-evident intuition. The libido or the will to
power in actuality constitutes a psycho-biologi-
cal residue which is not clear in itself and
which does not appear to us as *being before-
hand* the irreducible limit of the investigation.
Finally it is experience which establishes that
the foundation of complexes is this libido or
this will to power; and these results of empirical inquiry are perfectly contingent, they are
not convincing. Nothing prevents our conceiving *a priori* of a "human reality" which
would not be expressed by the will to power,
for which the libido would not constitute the
original, undifferentiated project.

On the other hand, the choice to which existential psychoanalysis will lead us, precisely
because it is a choice, accounts for its original
contingency, for the contingency of the choice
is the reverse side of its freedom. Furthermore, inasmuch as it is established on the *lack
of being,* conceived as a fundamental characteristic of being, it receives its legitimacy *as a
choice,* and we know that we do not have to
push further. Each result then will be at once
fully contingent and legitimately irreducible.
Moreover it will always remain *particular;* that
is, we will not achieve as the ultimate goal of

our investigation and the foundation of all behavior an abstract, general term, libido for example, which would be differentiated and made concrete first in complexes and then in detailed acts of conduct, due to the action of external facts and the history of the subject. On the contrary, it will be a choice which remains unique and which is from the start absolute concreteness. Details of behavior can express or *particularize* this choice, but they can not make it more concrete than is already known in a self-evident intuition. The libido or the will to power is in us. That is because the choice is nothing other than the being of each human reality; this amounts to saying that a particular partial behavior *is* or expresses the original choice of this human reality since for human reality there is no difference between existing and choosing for itself. From this fact we understand that existential psychoanalysis does not have to proceed from the fundamental "complex," which is exactly the choice of being, to an abstraction like the libido which would explain it. The complex is the ultimate choice, it is the choice of being and *makes itself such*. Bringing it into the light will reveal it each time as evidently irreducible. It follows necessarily that the libido and the will to power will appear to existential psychoanalysis neither as general characteristics common to all mankind nor as irreducibles. At most it will be possible after the investigation to establish that they express by virtue of particular ensembles in certain subjects a fundamental choice which can not be reduced to either one of them. We have seen in fact that desire and sexuality in general express an original effort of the for-itself to recover its being which has become estranged through contact with the Other. The will to power also originally supposes being-for-others, the comprehension of the Other, and the choice of winning its own salvation by means of the Other. The foundation of this attitude must be an original choice which would make us understand the radical identification of being-in-itself-for-itself with being-for-others.

The fact that the ultimate term of this existential inquiry must be a *choice,* distinguishes even better the psychoanalysis for which we have outlined the method and principal features. It thereby abandons the supposition that the environment acts mechanically on the subject under consideration. The environment can act on the subject only to the exact extent that he comprehends it; that is, transforms it into a situation. Hence no objective description of this environment could be of any use to us. From the start the environment conceived as a situation refers to the for-itself which is choosing, just as the for-itself refers to the environment by the very fact that the for-itself is in the world. By renouncing all mechanical causation, we renounce at the same time all *general* interpretation of the symbolization confronted. Our goal could not be to establish empirical laws of succession, nor could we constitute a universal symbolism. Rather the psychoanalyst will have to rediscover at each step a symbol functioning in the particular case which he is considering. If each being is a totality, it is not conceivable that there can exist elementary symbolic relationships (*e.g.*, the faeces = gold, or a pincushion = the breast) which preserve a constant meaning in all cases; that is, which remain unaltered when they pass from one meaningful ensemble to another ensemble. Furthermore the psychoanalyst will never lose sight of the fact that the choice is living and consequently can be revoked by the subject who is being studied. We have shown in the preceding chapter the importance of the *instant*, which represents abrupt changes in orientation and the assuming of a new position in the face of an unalterable past. From this moment on, we must always be ready to consider that symbols change meaning and to abandon the symbol used hitherto. Thus existential psychoanalysis will have to be completely flexible and adapt itself to the slightest observable changes in the subject. Our concern here is to understand what is *individual* and often even instantaneous. The method which has served for one subject will not necessarily be suitable to use for another subject or for the same subject at a later period.

Precisely because the goal of the inquiry must be to discover a *choice* and not a *state,* the investigator must recall on every occasion that his object is not a datum buried in the darkness of the unconscious but a free, conscious determination—which is not even resident in consciousness, but which is one with this consciousness itself. Empirical psychoanalysis, to the extent that its method is better than its principles, is often in sight of an existential discovery, but it always stops part way. When it thus approaches the fundamental choice, the resistance of the subject collapses suddenly and he *recognizes* the image of himself which is presented to him as if he were seeing himself in a mirror. This involuntary testimony of the subject is precious for the psychoanalyst; he sees there the sign that he has reached his goal; he can pass on from the investigation proper to the cure. But nothing in his principles or in his initial postulates permits him to understand or to utilize this testimony. Where could he get any such

right? If the complex is really unconscious—
that is, if there is a barrier separating the sign
from the thing signified—how could the subject *recognize* it? Does the unconscious complex
recognize itself? But haven't we been told that
it lacks *understanding*? And if of necessity we
granted to it the faculty of understanding the
signs, would this not be to make of it by the
same token a conscious unconscious? What is
understanding if not to be conscious of what is
understood? Shall we say on the other hand that
it is the subject as conscious who recognizes the
image presented? But how could he compare
it with his true state since that is out of reach
and since he has never had any knowledge of
it? At most he will be able to judge that the
psychoanalytic explanation of his case is a
probable hypothesis, which derives its probability from the number of behavior patterns
which it explains. His relation to this interpretation is that of a third party, that of the
psychoanalyst himself; he has no privileged
position. And if he *believes* in the probability
of the psychoanalytic hypothesis, is this simple
belief, which lives in the limits of his consciousness, able to effect the breakdown of the
barriers which dam up the unconscious tendencies? The psychoanalyst doubtless has some
obscure picture of an abrupt coincidence of
conscious and unconscious. But he has removed

all methods of conceiving of this coincidence in any positive sense.

Still, the enlightenment of the subject is a fact. There is an intuition here which is accompanied by evidence. The subject guided by the psychoanalyst does more and better than to give his agreement to an hypothesis; he touches it, he sees what it is. This is truly understandable only if the subject has never ceased being conscious of his deep tendencies; better yet, only if these drives are not distinguished from his conscious self. In this case as we have seen, the traditional psychoanalytic interpretation does not cause him to attain *consciousness* of what he is; it causes him to attain *knowledge* of what he is. It is existential psychoanalysis then which claims the final intuition of the subject as decisive.

This comparison allows us to understand better what an existential psychoanalysis must be if it is entitled to exist. It is a method destined to bring to light, in a strictly objective form, the subjective choice by which each living person makes himself a person; that is, makes known to himself what he is. Since what the method seeks is a *choice of being* at the same time as a *being*, it must reduce particular behavior patterns to fundamental relations—not of sexuality or of the will to power, but *of being*—which are expressed in this behavior.

It is then guided from the start toward a comprehension of being and must not assign itself any other goal than to discover being and the mode of being of the being confronting this being. It is forbidden to stop before attaining this goal. It will utilize the comprehension of being which characterizes the investigator inasmuch as he is himself a human reality; and as it seeks to detach being from its symbolic expressions, it will have to rediscover each time on the basis of a comparative study of acts and attitudes, a symbol destined to decipher them. Its criterion of success will be the number of facts which its hypothesis permits it to explain and to unify as well as the self-evident intuition of the irreducibility of the end attained. To this criterion will be added in all cases where it is possible, the decisive testimony of the subject. The results thus achieved—that is, the ultimate ends of the individual—can then become the object of a classification, and it is by the comparison of these results that we will be able to establish general considerations about human reality as an empirical choice of its own ends. The behavior studied by this psychoanalysis will include not only dreams, failures, obsessions, and neuroses, but also and especially the thoughts of waking life, successfully adjusted acts, style, *etc.* This psychoanalysis has not yet found its Freud. At most we can find the foreshadowing of it in certain particularly successful biographies. We hope to be able to attempt elsewhere two examples in relation to Flaubert and Dostoevsky. But it matters little to us whether it now exists; the important thing is that it is possible.

THE HOLE

IN ITSELF the *hole* is the symbol of a mode of being which existential psychoanalysis must elucidate.

We can not make such a detailed study here. One can see at once, however, that the hole is originally presented as a nothingness "to be filled" with my own flesh; the child can not restrain himself from putting his finger or his whole arm into the hole. It presents itself to me as the empty image of myself. I have only to crawl into it in order to make myself exist in the world which awaits me. The ideal of the hole is then an excavation which can be carefully moulded about my flesh in such a manner that by squeezing myself into it and fitting myself tightly inside it, I shall contribute to making a fullness of being exist in the world. Thus to plug up a hole means originally to make a sacrifice of my body in order that the plenitude of being may exist; that is, to subject the passion of the For-itself so as to shape, to perfect, and to preserve the totality of the In-itself.*

* We should note as well the importance of the opposite tendency, to poke through holes, which in itself demands an existential analysis.

Here at its origin we grasp one of the most fundamental tendencies of human reality—the tendency to fill. We shall meet with this tendency again in the adolescent and in the adult. A good part of our life is passed in plugging up holes, in filling empty places, in realizing and symbolically establishing a plenitude. The child recognizes as the results of his first experiences that he himself has holes. When he puts his fingers in his mouth, he tries to wall up the holes in his face; he expects that his finger will merge with his lips and the roof of his mouth and block up the buccal orifice as one fills the crack in a wall with cement; he seeks again the density, the uniform and spherical plenitude of Parmenidean being; if he sucks his thumb, it is precisely in order to dissolve it, to transform it into a sticky paste which will seal the hole of his mouth. This tendency is certainly one of the most fundamental among those which serve as the basis for the act of eating; nourishment is the "cement" which will seal the mouth; to eat is among other things to be filled up.

It is only from this standpoint that we can pass on to sexuality. The obscenity of the feminine sex is that of everything which "gapes open." It is *an appeal to being* as all holes are. In herself woman appeals to a strange flesh which is to transform her into a fullness of being by penetration and dissolution. Conversely woman senses her condition as an appeal precisely because she is "in the form of a hole." This is the true origin of Adler's complex. Beyond any doubt her sex is a mouth and a voracious mouth which devours the penis—a fact which can easily lead to the idea of castration. The amorous act is the castration of the man; but this is above all because sex is a hole. We have to do here with a *pre-sexual* contribution which will become one of the components of sexuality as an empirical, complex, human attitude but which far from deriving its origin from the sexed being has nothing in common with basic sexuality, the nature of which we have explained in Part III. Nevertheless the experience with the hole, when the infant sees the reality, includes the ontological presentiment of sexual experience in general; it is with his flesh that the child stops up the hole and the hole, before all sexual specification, is an obscene expectation, an appeal to the flesh.

We can see the importance which the elucidation of these immediate and concrete existential categories will assume for existential psychoanalysis. In this way we can apprehend the very general projects of human reality. But what chiefly interests the psychoanalyst is to determine the free project of the unique person in terms of the individual relation which

unites him to these various symbols of being. I
can love slimy contacts, have a horror of holes,
etc. That does not mean that for me the slimy,
the greasy, a hole, *etc.* have lost their general
ontological meaning, but on the contrary that
because of this meaning, I determine myself in
this or that manner in relation to them. If the
slimy is indeed the symbol of a being in which
the for-itself is swallowed up by the in-itself,
what kind of a person am I if in encountering
others, I love the slimy? To what fundamental
project of myself am I referred if I want to explain this love of an ambiguous, sucking in-itself? In this way *tastes* do not remain irreducible givens; if one knows how to question them,
they reveal to us the fundamental projects of
the person. Down to even our alimentary pref-
erences they all have a meaning. We can account for this fact if we will reflect that each
taste is presented, not as an absurd *datum* which
we must excuse but as an evident value. If I
like the taste of garlic, it seems irrational to
me that other people can not like it.

To eat is to appropriate by destruction; it
is at the same time to be filled up with a certain
being. And this being is given as a synthesis
of temperature, density, and flavor proper.
In a word this synthesis signifies *a certain
being;* and when we eat, we do not limit
ourselves to *knowing* certain qualities of this

being through taste; by tasting them we appropriate them. Taste is assimilation; by the very act of biting the tooth reveals the density of a body which it is transforming into gastric contents. Thus the synthetic intuition of food is in itself an assimilative destruction. It reveals to me the being which I am going to make my flesh. Henceforth, what I accept or what I reject with disgust is the very being of that existent, or if you prefer, the totality of the food proposes to me a certain mode of being of the being which I accept or refuse. This totality is organized as a form in which less intense qualities of density and of temperature are effaced behind the flavor proper which *expresses* them. The *sugary*, for example, *expresses* the slimy when we eat a spoonful of honey or molasses, just as an analytical function expresses a geometric curve. This means that all qualities which are not strictly speaking flavor but which are massed, melted, buried in the flavor, represent the *matter* of the flavor. (The piece of chocolate which at first offers a resistance to my tooth, soon abruptly gives way and crumbles; its resistance first, then its crumbling *is* chocolate.) In addition they are united to certain temporal characteristics of flavor; that is, to its mode of temporalization. Certain tastes give themselves all at once, some are like delayed-action fuses, some release themselves by degrees, certain ones dwindle slowly until they disappear, and still others vanish at the very moment one thinks to possess them. These qualities are organized along with density and temperature; in addition on another level they express the visual aspect of the food. If I eat a pink cake, the taste of it is pink; the light sugary perfume, the oiliness of the butter cream *are* the pink. Thus I eat the pink as I see the sugary. We conclude that flavor, due to this fact, has a complex architecture and differentiated matter; it is this structured matter—which represents for us a particular type of being—that we can assimilate or reject with nausea, according to our original project. It is not a matter of indifference whether we like oysters or clams, snails or shrimp, if only we know how to unravel the existential significance of these foods.

Generally speaking there is no irreducible taste or inclination. They all represent a certain appropriative choice of being. It is up to existential psychoanalysis to compare and classify them. Ontology abandons us here; it has merely enabled us to determine the ultimate ends of human reality, its fundamental possibilities, and the value which haunts it. Each human reality is at the same time a direct project to metamorphose its own For-itself into an In-itself-For-itself and a project of the appropriation of the world as a totality of being-in-itself, in the form of a fundamental quality. Every human reality is a passion in that it projects losing itself so as to found being and by the same stroke to constitute the In-itself which escapes contingency by being its own foundation, the *Ens causa sui,* which religions call God. Thus the passion of man is the reverse of that of Christ, for man loses himself as man in order that God may be born. But the idea of God is contradictory and we lose ourselves in vain. Man is a useless passion.

ETHICAL IMPLICATIONS

ONTOLOGY itself can not formulate ethical pre-
cepts. It is concerned solely with what is, and
we can not possibly derive imperatives from
ontology's indicatives. It does, however, allow
us to catch a glimpse of what sort of ethics will
assume its responsibilities when confronted
with a *human reality in situation.* Ontology has
revealed to us, in fact, the origin and the nature of *value;* we have seen that value is the
lack in relation to which the for-itself determines its being as *a lack.* By the very fact that
the for-itself *exists,* as we have seen, value arises
to haunt its being-for-itself. It follows that the
various tasks of the for-itself can be made the
object of an existential psychoanalysis, for
they all aim at producing the missing synthesis
of consciousness and being in the form of value
or self-cause. Thus existential psychoanalysis is
moral description, for it releases to us the
ethical meaning of various human projects. It
indicates to us the necessity of abandoning the
psychology of interest along with any utilita-
rian interpretation of human conduct—by revealing to us the *ideal* meaning of all human
attitudes. These meanings are beyond egoism

and altruism, beyond also any behavior which is called *disinterested*. Man makes himself man in order to be God, and selfness considered from this point of view can appear to be an egoism; but precisely because there is no common measure between human reality and the self-cause which it wants to be, one could just as well say that man loses himself in order that the self-cause may exist. We will consider then that all human existence is a passion, the famous *self-interest* being only one way freely chosen among others to realize this passion.

But the principal result of existential psychoanalysis must be to make us repudiate the *spirit of seriousness*. The spirit of seriousness has two characteristics: it considers values as transcendent givens independent of human subjectivity, and it transfers the quality of "desirable" from the ontological structure of things to their simple material constitution. For the spirit of seriousness, for example, *bread* is desirable because it is *necessary* to live (a value written in an intelligible heaven) and because bread *is* nourishing. The result of the serious attitude, which as we know rules the world, is to cause the symbolic values of things to be drunk in by their empirical idiosyncrasy as ink by a blotter; it puts forward the opacity of the desired object and posits it in itself as a desirable irreducible. Thus we are already on the moral plane but concurrently on that of bad faith, for it is an ethics which is ashamed of itself and does not dare speak its name. It has obscured all its goals in order to free itself from anguish. Man pursues being blindly by hiding from himself the free project which is this pursuit. He makes himself such that he is *waited for* by all the tasks placed along his way. Objects are mute demands, and he is nothing in himself but the passive obedience to these demands.

Existential psychoanalysis is going to reveal to man the real goal of his pursuit, which is being as a synthetic fusion of the in-itself with the for-itself; existential psychoanalysis is going to acquaint man with his passion. In truth there are many men who have practiced this psychoanalysis on themselves and who have not waited to learn its principles in order to make use of them as a means of deliverance and salvation. Many men, in fact, know that the goal of their pursuit is being; and to the extent that they possess this knowledge, they refrain from appropriating things for their own sake and try to realize the symbolic appropriation of their being-in-itself. But to the extent that this attempt still shares in the spirit of seriousness and that these men can still believe that their mission of effecting the existence of the in-itself-for-itself is written in things, they are condemned to despair; for they discover at the same time that all human activities are equivalent (for they all tend to sacrifice man in order that the self-cause may arise) and that all are on principle doomed to failure. Thus it amounts to the same thing whether one gets drunk alone or is a leader of nations. If one of these activities takes precedence over the other, this will not be because of its real goal but because of the degree of consciousness which it possesses of its ideal goal; and in this case it will be the quietism of the solitary drunkard which will take precedence over the vain agitation of the leader of nations.

But ontology and existential psychoanalysis (or the spontaneous and empirical application which men have always made of these disciplines) must reveal to the moral agent that he is *the being by whom values exist*. It is then that his freedom will become conscious of itself and will reveal itself in anguish as the unique source of value and the nothingness by which the *world* exists. As soon as freedom discovers the quest for being and the appropriation of the in-itself as *its own possibles,* it will apprehend by and in anguish that they are possibles only on the ground of the possibility of other possibles. But hitherto although possibles could be chosen and rejected *ad libitum,* the theme which made the unity of all choices of possibles was the value or the ideal presence of the *ens causa sui.* What will become of freedom if it turns its back upon this value? Will freedom carry this value along with it whatever it does and even in its very turning back upon this value? Will freedom carry this value along with it whatever it does and even in its very turning back upon the in-itself-for-itself? Will freedom be reapprehended from behind by the value which it wishes to contemplate? Or will freedom by the very fact that it apprehends itself as a freedom in relation to itself, be able to put an end to the reign of this value? In particular is it possible for freedom to take itself for a value as the source of all value, or must it necessarily be defined in relation to a transcendent value which haunts it? And in case it could will itself as its own possible and its determining value, what would this mean? A freedom which wills itself freedom is in fact a being-which-is-not-what-it-is and which-is-what-it-is-not, and which chooses as the ideal of being, being-what-it-is-not and not-being-what-it-is.

This freedom chooses then not to recover itself but to flee itself, not to coincide with itself but to be always at a distance *from* itself. What are we to understand by this being which wills to hold itself in awe, to be at a distance from itself? Is it a question of bad faith or of another fundamental attitude? And can one *live* this new aspect of being? In particular will freedom by taking itself for an end escape all *situation?* Or on the contrary, will it remain situated? Or will it situate itself so much the more precisely and the more individually as it projects itself further in anguish as a conditioned freedom and accepts more fully its responsibility as an existent by whom the world comes into being. All these questions, which refer us to a pure and not an accessory reflection, can find their reply only on the ethical plane. We shall devote to them a future work.